Someone Should Have Told Me

by Holly-ann Martin

Someone Should Have Told Me
by Holly-ann Martin

Published March 2018
by Safe 4 Kids (Aust) Pty Ltd
www.safe4kids.com.au
PO Box 367
Armadale WA 6992
Australia
©2018 Safe4Kids

This publication contains the opinions and ideas of its author. It is intended to provide helpful and informative material on the subject matter covered. It is not intended to replace professional services and is offered in good faith for the purpose of raising awareness and in an advisory capacity only.

While the book has been written in good faith, the author and publisher assume no responsibility for any liability, loss, or risk, personal or otherwise, which is incurred as a consequence, directly or indirectly, of the use and application of any of the contents of this book.

All rights reserved. No part of this book may be reproduced, stored in a retrieval system or transmitted by any means, e.g. mechanical, electronic, photocopying, recording or otherwise, without written permission from the author.

Illustrations by Marilyn Fahie
Cover designed by Steve Horton

Printed by CreateSpace,
an Amazon.com Company

A catalogue record for this book is available from the National Library of Australia

ISBN: 978-0-6482877-0-4 (paperback)

This is not a children's book. This is a book designed for adults to share with children, to start conversations about some sensitive topics. I recommend you read this book first before you share it with your children.

I dedicate this book to my fantastic illustrator Marilyn Fahie, whose magnificent drawings brought my words to life.

I would also like to thank Cath Hakanson without whose persistent encouragement I would never have written this book.

I wish someone had told me not to type private words into the computer.

Someone should have told me
I might see private things on
video sites.

Why didn't someone tell me not to talk

even if they seem

to people I didn't know on the computer,
friendly and look nice?

I wish somebody had told me that, if I hear other children talking about private things they have seen, I should walk away and tell a grown-up.

Someone should have told me not to click on pop-ups when I'm playing online.

Why didn't someone tell me that not all cartoons are suitable for children? Some cartoons can be private too.

I wish someone had told me not to let other people take pictures of my private body parts.

Someone should have told me not to take pictures of my own private body parts because it's against the law.

Why didn't somebody tell me not to go online when my grown-ups were asleep?

Well, I'm going to tell you what you really need to know about the internet.

Private pictures or private movies show people's private body parts or people doing private things.

You might hear some people call these kinds of pictures or movies "porn", "porno", "pornography", "nudes" or "sexting".

You can come across these pictures or movies by accident or friends, other kids, teens or adults could show them to you.

If you come across private pictures, you should tell a grown-up straight away. You mustn't show these pictures to any other kids.

If you see private pictures or private movies you should close your eyes or turn away and say, "That's private," out loud, then go and tell an adult.

If you see private pictures or private movies try to think of something that you like to watch or do, and not think about the things that you saw.

The Internet is a wonderful place, but there can be dangers, and if you feel unsafe, just as in the real world, you need to tell a grown-up.

Information for Parents, Carers and Teachers

As parents, carers, and teachers, we try to protect children from online dangers, including exposure to graphic, hard-core pornography, people who groom children and violent content. Unfortunately, with children able to access mobile devices at ever earlier ages, this is becoming increasingly difficult. It is no longer a question of *if* your child comes across pornography or other inappropriate content, but *when*. It is crucially important that both adults and children are educated about the potential impact of early exposure to pornography, about people who prey on children, about adult content and what actions they need to take.

DISCUSSION QUESTIONS

Below is additional information on each of the potential dangers covered in the book and questions you can ask children to see if they have understood the key concepts. These discussion questions will also give you the opportunity to provide further information if required, which is appropriate to the comprehension level of the children you are working with.

The page numbers next to each discussion question indicate where that topic is in the book. This will allow you to revisit that page with children before commencing each discussion question.

PAGE 4 Discuss with your child that it is normal to want to know about their private body parts, but going online can lead to them seeing things that children shouldn't see. Think back to when you were a child, you might have looked up "sex" in the dictionary. Well, nowadays dictionaries are out, and Google is in, and if your child types in anything they hear either in the playground, on the bus, on the television or even from overhearing an adult conversation, they may be exposed to some very graphic adult content. Please encourage your child to come to you first before googling ANYTHING, reassuring them they can talk with you about anything and if you don't know the answer you will do your best to find out and let them know. A child can't "unsee" these images.

Questions you could ask:

- Where could you search for private words apart from Google? (YouTube, Wikipedia, etc.)
- What other technology could you use? (Tablets, phones, etc.)

PAGE 5 Discuss with your child that not all of the content on video sharing sites is suitable for them. Pornography is one of the main concerns; however, there are other types of video content which may have a negative impact on children. One example is videos that show parents playing pranks on their children. Some parents play very mean tricks on their kids, and the children can suffer emotional distress as a result of these pranks. Children who watch these videos may also become distressed.

Remember to use safe search filters for search engines. If you are happy for your child to use the adult version of YouTube, keep in mind it has a rating of 13 years+ due to a large amount of adult content.

Questions you could ask:

- What kinds of things might you see on video sharing sites?
- Have you ever seen something that made you feel uncomfortable?

PAGES 6 & 7 Discuss with your child that, just as they wouldn't talk to a stranger in the real world, they shouldn't talk to people they don't know online. A person you meet online may look nice and even sound nice, but they may not actually be who you think they are, or who they pretend to be. One way online strangers make contact with children is while they are online gaming. Adults pretend to be children to gain children's trust and then they start to groom them. Tell your child to be mindful of anyone who asks them for personal information — their name, address, email, phone number, hobbies, other interests or which school they attend. Anything that can identify your child. Also make sure your child uses an avatar, rather than a picture of themselves.

Questions you could ask:

- Has anyone ever said anything inappropriate to you while you were playing on the computer?
- Have you ever been asked personal questions?

PAGE 8 Discuss with your child that they may hear other children – often older children or adults – talking about private things (pornography) they have seen or heard about. This can distress children and may even give them nightmares. If they hear anyone talking about private things such as pornography, they should walk away and tell an adult they trust who can help them.

Questions you could ask:

- How do you think the boys sitting on the bench listening are feeling?
- Have you ever heard your friends, other kids, teenagers or adults talking about things that you didn't understand or that made you feel uncomfortable?

PAGE 9 Discuss with your child that pop-ups may occur when they are playing games, looking up information or viewing videos on YouTube or other video sharing sites. These pop-ups might be a box that appears, an icon that is flashing, saying you are a winner, or many other tricks designed to gain a child's attention. However, children should not click on any of these, as they may see unsuitable content. Teach them not to download anything without asking you first, as these downloads may contain viruses or adult content.

Questions you could ask:

- Have you ever clicked on a pop-up?
- If yes, what happened when you clicked on the pop-up?

PAGE 10 Discuss with your child that not all cartoons and animations are suitable for children. There are people who try to shock children with content that isn't suitable for them. Anime is a type of Japanese animation that has colourful graphics and vibrant characters, with fantasy themes which can appeal to young people yet may contain adult content. Children can be drawn to it because it's colourful and pretty, but it may contain content unsuitable for children.

Questions you could ask:

- Have you ever seen cartoons with private things in them?
- If yes, how did it make you feel?

PAGE 11 Discuss grooming behaviours with your child. Grooming is when someone befriends a child to gain their trust so they can take advantage of the child. People who prey on children use very sophisticated tactics. Discuss how the man on page 11 might have said to the young boy "Oh, you look so handsome in that Superman outfit; let's take some photos of you", then after a while, "How about we get some action shots of you bouncing on the bed?" The boy knows he is not allowed to bounce on the bed, but the man says, "It will be our little secret", all the time normalising what they are doing, and blurring the rules. Once he has control of the boy, he might say, "I know what would be really funny. How about you take your clothes off and just leave your Superman cape on?" Children can be groomed by strangers or by somebody they know and trust.

Questions you could ask:

- What are your private body parts?
- Do you know the correct names for your private body parts?
- Has anyone ever taken pictures of your private body parts?
- Why do you think someone might want to take private pictures?

PAGE 12 Discuss with your child that grooming can be face-to-face and can also occur online. A person who preys on children wants to lower the child's inhibitions by breaking down the boundaries. While being groomed online, children may be persuaded to share nude or indecent images (pictures or movies) of themselves or live stream via web-cam. Make a rule that they must never send any private pictures or private movies to anyone! This rule can be extended to not allowing children to send any type of pictures or movies to people they don't know in real life, without checking with you first. Also, talk with your child about what to do if anyone sends them private pictures or private movies; reassure them that they need to tell an adult they trust and that you won't take away their device or punish them.

Questions you could ask:

- Have you ever taken pictures like that?
- Have you ever been asked to send private pictures?
- What would you do if someone sent you pictures of their private body parts?

PAGE 13 Discuss with your child the dangers of going online unsupervised. Children aged from eight years admit they go online while their parents are asleep. Explain to your child the potential dangers of online predators and viewing adult content. If someone makes them feel uncomfortable or they get their Early Warning Signs from something they have viewed, they need to tell someone on their Safety Team. You might want to have a family rule that technology is never allowed in bedrooms and especially overnight. (For information on Early Warning Signs and Safety Teams, see pages 25 and 26).

Questions you could ask:

- Have you ever gone online while I was asleep?
- What could happen if you go online when I'm asleep?

PAGE 15   Discuss with your child what pornography, nudes and sexting are. These are private pictures or private movies that show people's private body parts or people doing private adult things. You may hear people also using words like *porn* or *porno*; they all mean the same thing. People need to be over 18 years of age to view these kinds of pictures or movies because children's brains are still growing and it's not healthy for them. You might tell your child – "You need to put healthy food in your body to grow up big and strong and healthy pictures in your mind so that it is also big and strong. Seeing these kinds of private pictures or private movies can make you feel uncomfortable, upset and even give you nightmares. On the other hand, you might find it confusing because you feel excited and interested. That is totally normal, but children are not ready for those kinds of feelings yet."

Questions you could ask:

- Who would you talk to if you saw private pictures or private movies?
- Have you heard words like *pornography*, *porn*, *porno*, *nudes* or *sexting* before?

PAGE 16   Discuss with your child that they can come across all kinds of unsuitable content by accident on the internet. Your friends, other kids, teens and even adults may try to share inappropriate content with them. It is very common for somebody trying to groom a child to use language like "let's play a little game" in order to produce particular sexualised behaviours. It can be very subtle and difficult for children to recognise.

Questions you could ask:

- What do you think grooming is?
- Who might groom children?

PAGE 17   Discuss with your child that "they can talk with you about anything"; that no subject is off limits. For example, they might have received mean or strange messages, people might have been swearing, or they have been asked for private information while playing a game online or seen something private or upsetting. Reassure your child that they can talk with you and you will try and help them. It is also important they understand you will not take their device away. Fear of having their device taken and shame are the two main reasons children don't disclose when things like this happen.

Questions you could ask:

- Who else could you talk to, if I wasn't around or busy?
- Who are five people you could talk to?

PAGE 18   Discuss with your child that if they do see private pictures or private movies they should close their eyes or turn away and say, "That's private," out loud, then go and tell an adult. If they see private pictures or private movies on an iPad they should turn it over; if it's on a computer just turn off the screen, not the whole computer, or simply turn their head so they can't see it. If possible, they should show you what they have seen without looking at it again, which is why they should just turn off the computer screen or turn the iPad over rather than turn it off. If they are asked to describe what they have seen, children may play it down to avoid getting into trouble, and also we don't want them trying to remember it, as it may re-traumatise them, particularly if they have viewed hard-core pornography. If they think they will be tempted to look at it again, then they should turn it off.

Questions you could ask:

- Have you ever seen private pictures or private movies?

- If yes, what did you do?
- How did it make you feel?

`PAGE 19` Discuss with your child that if they see something that makes them feel unsafe or uncomfortable, they should try and think of something they would rather watch or do. Explain it is like trying to reboot their brain, because many children can have flashbacks and nightmares after seeing content that they are not mature enough to understand and process.

A question you could ask:

- If you saw something that made you feel unsafe what would you think about?

WHAT TO DO IF YOUR CHILD HAS SEEN PORNOGRAPHY

STAY CALM AND LISTEN: If your child confides in you, or you find out they have seen pornography, ensure your reaction is controlled and measured. It is important that you do not overreact and close down the conversation with your child. The way you communicate with your child will not only determine how comfortable they are in speaking with you about it further but will also provide you with information about what it is they have actually seen.

Let them know you aren't angry with them (you may be disappointed), and reassure them that you are glad that you know, so you can help them make sense of what they saw. If you find yourself upset at any point in the conversation, reassure your child you aren't angry with them but simply upset at the situation. This will encourage your child to trust you and continue speaking with you.

GATHER INFORMATION: Ask them how they came to see these pictures or movies. Perhaps it was an accident, or maybe they were curious and went searching for information. If someone else has shown them, let them know that it's okay for them to tell you who that person was, and if possible how old they were. Explain to your child it is against the law for anyone to show them private pictures or private movies. Discuss that the law says you need to be over 18 years of age to look at pictures or movies like these.

Determine if your child is regularly viewing pornography or if this was a one-off event. If they have developed a habit of frequently viewing pornography, you may like to consider seeking professional help.

REASSURE: Our children need to know they can come to us if they have any questions at all. They need to be reassured that they have done the right thing in telling you (or admitting they have seen pornography) and be encouraged to keep the lines of communication open for the future.

Try to steer clear of punishments such as removing devices, because this may cause shame and confusion, particularly if your child has viewed the pornography by accident. You may need to create new rules about device usage. For example, mobile phones, tablets, and computers are not allowed in bedrooms, and there are set time frames in which these devices can be used. This is good practise to manage all forms of cyber safety.

You may want to speak with your child about your own experiences if you saw private pictures or movies as a child. As you speak, watch them for any indication they may need to continue to discuss and process what they have seen.

Children are naturally curious about bodies, sex, and the creation of babies. However, they do need to learn about it in a gradual and age-appropriate manner. Let them know that curiosity is okay, and encourage them to come and ask you questions about anything, at any time. There are many great resources available for parents to help them talk to their kids about sex.

It is possible your child may use the internet to find out more about their bodies, sex, and the creation of babies, and find themselves viewing content that is upsetting and inappropriate. Encourage your child to come and tell you if they see any private pictures or private movies, or if someone ever tries to show them pornographic images.

ADDITIONAL INFORMATION

Below is an introduction to some of the core concepts of the *Safe4Kids Protective Education Program*. It is important children have an understanding of these concepts to help keep them safe.

FEELINGS: When children are asked to name feelings or talk about their feelings, they find it difficult because they are not familiar with those words. Children need to understand that all feelings are okay; it's the negative behaviours that go with some feelings that are not acceptable. Everybody's feelings are different, and nobody can tell you how you should feel. Be mindful of saying to children, "Don't be scared," or "Don't be silly," when they show signs of distress or discomfort about something. Instead, brainstorm with children what they can do to make themselves feel safer if they are feeling a negative emotion.

EARLY WARNING SIGNS: Early Warning Signs are our body's way of telling us that we feel unsafe. They are our "fight, flight, or freeze" response. They are also known as our intuition or "gut feelings". Early Warning Signs can be different for each of us, and include sweaty palms, feeling unable to move, rapid heartbeat, butterflies in our tummy, goose bumps, hair on our arms standing up, etc.

SAFETY TEAM OR NETWORK: A Safety Team is five trusted adults a child can talk with if they feel unsafe. Children need to know that these trusted adults will:

- listen to them
- believe them
- be available to them and
- take action if necessary, to help them feel safe again.

Help your child develop a Safety Team who will provide support and help protect them.

PERSISTENCE: When children need help, they must be taught to persist, to keep on asking for help until they receive it. If a child needs help, the first person they approach will not always listen to them or be able to help them. Children need to persist and keep telling trusted adults on their Safety Team until their Early Warning Signs go away and they feel safe again. Persistence is of particular value in an emergency – when you need help immediately.

NAMES OF PRIVATE BODY PARTS: It is essential children are taught the correct anatomical names for their private body parts. Their private body parts are those parts covered by their bathers, and also their mouth. Boys' private body parts are mouth, bottom, penis and testicles. Girls' private body parts are mouth, breasts, bottom, vulva and vagina.

This is not sex education. It is merely teaching children the correct terminology so that if they are subjected to abuse, they can disclose the abuse using the correct private body parts names, which has proven very beneficial in assisting prosecutors. It is also a deterrent for perpetrators if a child can use the correct names for their private body parts since it is an indication that the child may have received some form of Protective Education.

SAYING "NO": Children are taught to respect their elders, to be polite and always to obey adults. Unfortunately, this can, and does, place them in harm's way. Children are often abused by people they know and trust. Children need to be taught that if they feel unsafe or have their Early Warning Signs, it is okay to say "No" to anyone, especially if someone tries to touch their private body parts. It is also okay to break the rules of politeness and expected behaviour. If there is an emergency, then it's okay to interrupt adults, to keep themselves safe or help someone else in danger.

SECRETS: Children need to know that there are two kinds of secrets:

"Good" or "Safe" secrets are only kept for a short time and will make someone happy when the secret is revealed. For example, a surprise birthday party, where everyone but the birthday person knows about the party for days or weeks in advance.

"Bad" or "Unsafe" secrets will make a child feel anxious, concerned or uncomfortable; they may have their Early Warning Signs. They will be told they must never tell, and that the secret must be kept for a long time, maybe even a lifetime. Unsafe secrets are kept by threats, coercion, bribes, and manipulation. Other ways children can identify a Bad or Unsafe Secret is that there may only be two people who know the secret. Children need to know they should never keep Bad or Unsafe secrets, and always to tell someone on their Safety Team. Teach children they should never keep a secret about any kind of touching, even if they like the touch or the secret little special game.

For more information on child protection education and resources visit www.safe4kids.com.au

RECEIVING A DISCLOSURE

If your child discloses that they have been abused, either physically, sexually or emotionally, here are some suggestions which may help your child, and you, to feel safe:

STAY CALM: Try to put your feelings aside, as an outraged reaction will only reinforce your child's reluctance to disclose. To help you stay calm and in control, try and remember the following three things you need to tell your child:

"I'm glad you told me"

"I believe you"

"It is not your fault".

BELIEVE YOUR CHILD: Children rarely lie about abuse, but they are often discouraged from disclosing because they think no one will believe them. It is therefore very important they know that you believe them.

OFFER REASSURANCE: Reassure your child that it is not their fault and they haven't done anything wrong; they are not to blame. You can also use phrases such as:

"You've done the right thing by telling me," or,

"I'm sorry this has happened to you, and we'll work this out together."

DO NOT QUESTION YOUR CHILD: Do not pressure your child to give in-depth details. They may have to repeat their story for authorities, and they may find it distressing each time they have to recount the abuse.

DO NOT APPROACH THE ALLEGED PERPETRATOR: Leave this to the authorities.

MAKE NO PROMISES: Do not promise to keep this a secret. You may have to tell the authorities about what has happened.

CONTACT AUTHORITIES

The Department for Child Protection

Police Child Protection Unit

OTHER CONTACTS:

Kids Helpline 1800 55 1800 (Australia only) or

www.kidshelpline.com.au

OTHER BOOKS BY THE AUTHOR

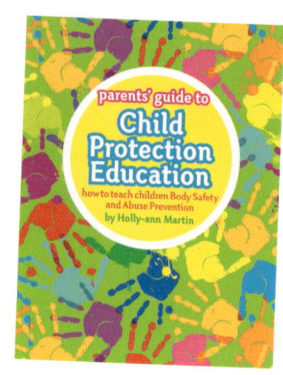

The *parents' guide to Child Protection Education* provides an informative, easy-to-follow holistic approach to teaching children abuse prevention education and includes activities to help children understand these important concepts.

Matilda learns a valuable lesson looks at unwanted touching (non-sexual) and teaches children if they feel unsafe they need to seek help from an adult they trust. If one adult doesn't listen, then they need to persist and tell another adult they trust and to keep telling until an adult helps them, and they feel safe again.

Hayden-Reece learns a valuable lesson that Private Means 'Just for you' teaches children the correct anatomical names for their private body parts and that no one should see or touch their private body parts without their consent. The book follows a logical progression and discusses public and private rooms, body functions, behaviours, language and clothing, and culminates in private body parts. It is essential children know the correct anatomical names for their private body parts as it can be a protective factor in deterring a potential perpetrator.

Hayden-Reece Learns What To Do if Children See Private Pictures or Private Movies. This book follows on from the first Hayden-Reece story. It revises the concept of public and private and then leads into the discussion on private pictures and private movies (pornography). This book provides both children and adults with strategies suggesting what to do if children view pornography either by accident, intentionally or are shown pornography by an adult or another child.

Gary just didn't know the rules helps parents, carers, and teachers address the issue of child-to-child sexual abuse. It is designed for adults to read to children to educate them about this subject in a safe, non-threatening manner and empowers children to help keep themselves safe. Included is information on how to respond to children engaged in problem sexual behaviours and also what to do if you receive a disclosure of abuse from a child.

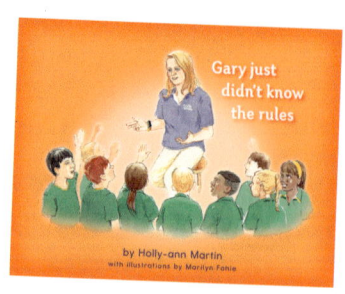

Made in the USA
Monee, IL
16 April 2026

48438897R10019